CONTENTS

Page	Title	Demo Track	Play-Along Track
2	Brain Stew (The Godzilla Remix) GREEN DAY	1	2
7	Empire QUEENSRYCHE	3	4
24	The Freshmen THE VERVE PIPE	5	6
33	Interstate Love Song STONE TEMPLE PILOTS	7	8
38	Mother DANZIG	9	10
45	Mr. Jones COUNTING CROWS	11	12
18	Push MATCHBOX 20	13	14
54	Yellow Ledbetter PEARL JAM	15	16
	TUNING NOTES	17	
63	GUITAR NOTATION LEGEND		

ISBN 978-1-4234-9684-7

HAL•LEONARD®
CORPORATION

7777 W. BLUEMOUND RD. P.O. BOX 13819 MILWAUKEE, WI 53213

Visit Hal Leonard Online at
www.halleonard.com

Brain Stew (The Godzilla Remix)

from the TriStar Motion Picture GODZILLA

Words by Billie Joe Armstrong
Music by Green Day

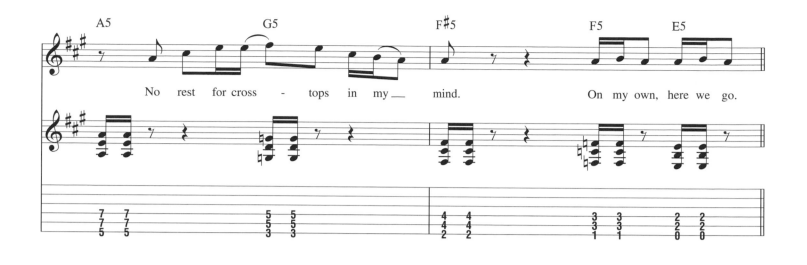

No rest for cross - tops in my __ mind. On my own, here we go.

Interlude

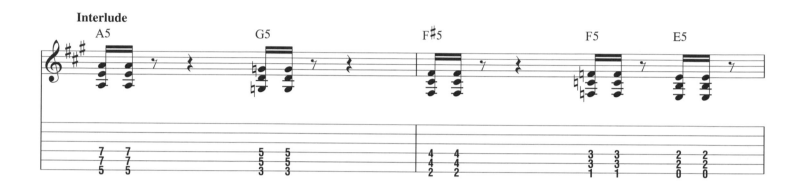

Verse

2., 4. My eyes feel like __ they're gon - na bleed. __
3. *See additional lyrics*

*Random harmonics produced while lightly muting on strings.

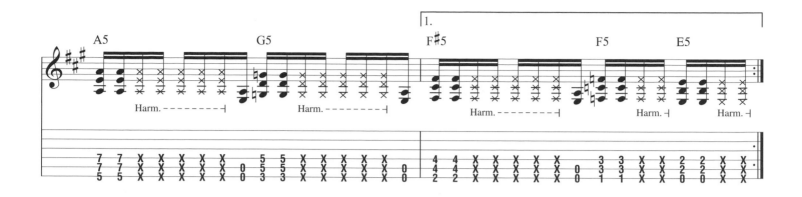

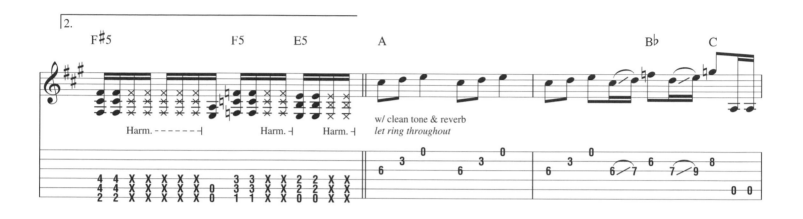

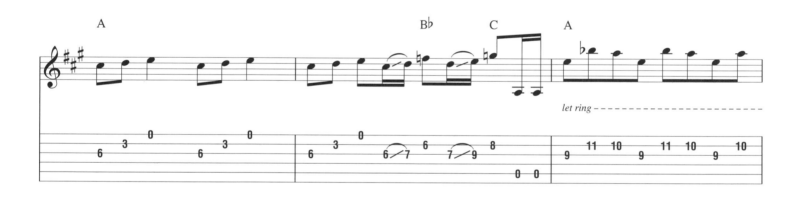

D.S. al Coda

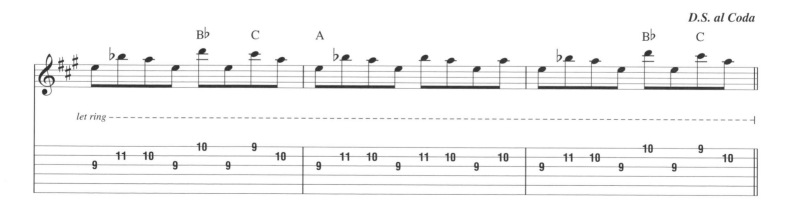

Coda

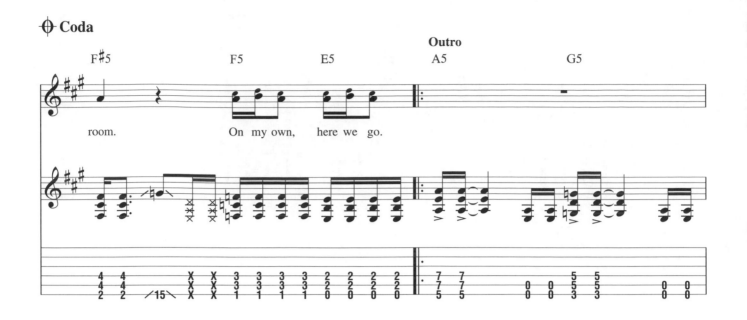

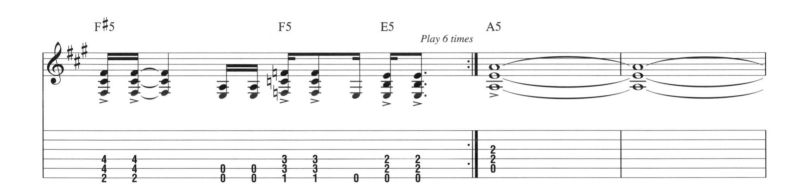

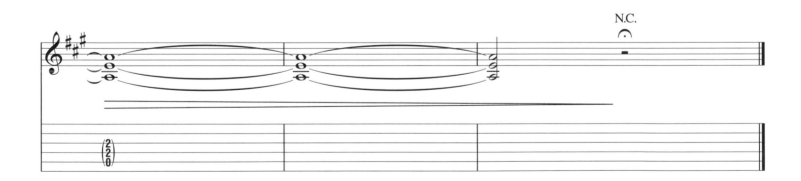

Additional Lyrics

3. My mind is set on overdrive.
   The clock is laughing in my face.
   Crooked spine, my senses dulled.
   Passed the point of delerium.
   On my own, here we go.

Empire

Words and Music by Geoff Tate and Michael Wilton

Intro
Moderately slow Rock ♩ = 80

Next message, saved, Saturday at 9:24 P.M. "Sorry, I'm just...it's starting to hit me like a, um, um, two ton heavy thing."

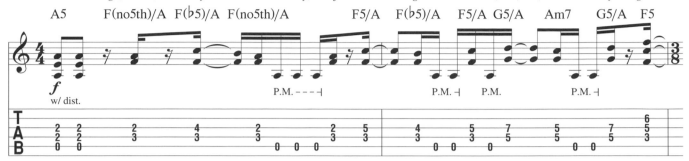

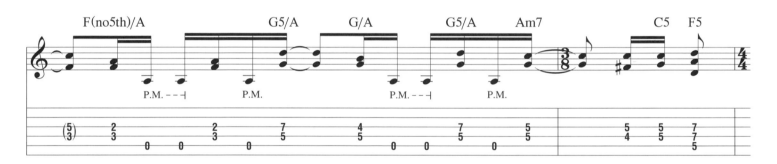

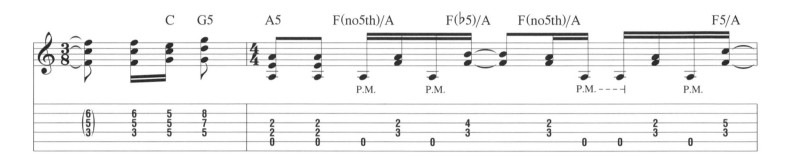

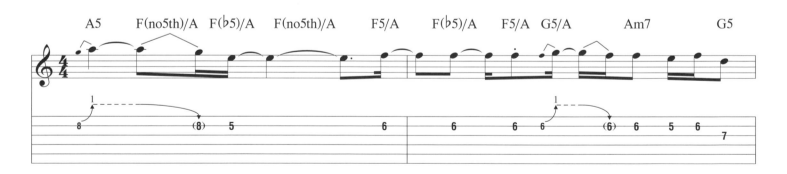

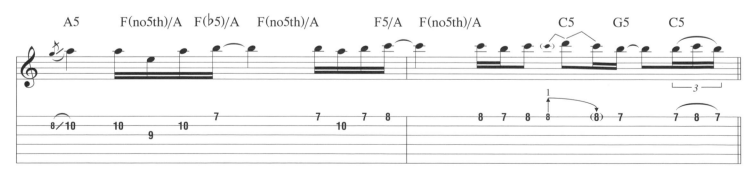

Verse

man, black man, trapped a-gain, __ holds his chains in his hand. __

Broth-er kill-ing broth-er for the prof-it of an-oth-er, __ game point, no-bod-y wins. __

De - clines _____ right on time. __ What hap-pened to the dream sub-lime? _____

Tear it all down, we'll build it up a-gain. __ An - oth - er em - pire?

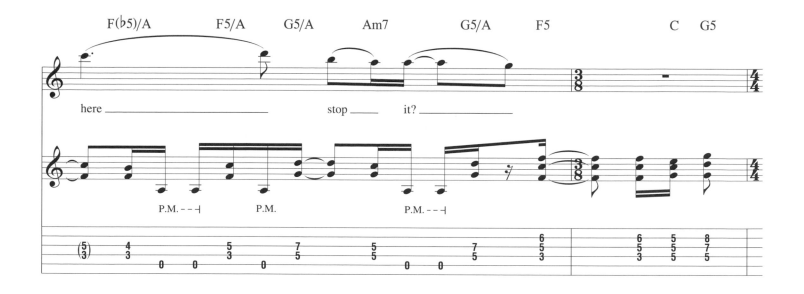

here _____ stop ____ it? _____

Interlude

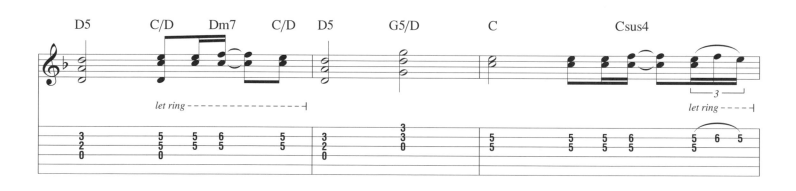

dist. off
w/ delay & chorus

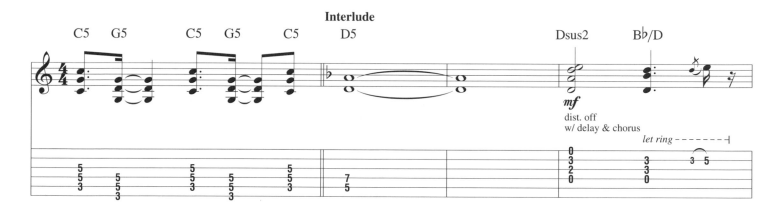

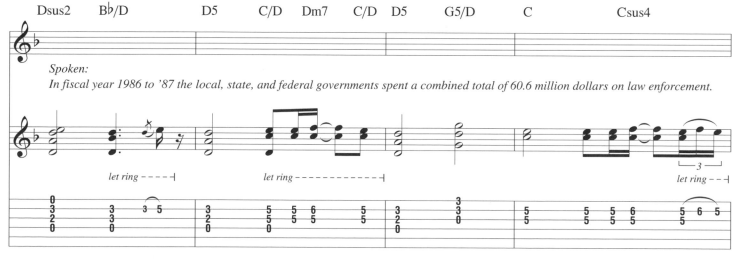

Spoken:
In fiscal year 1986 to '87 the local, state, and federal governments spent a combined total of 60.6 million dollars on law enforcement.

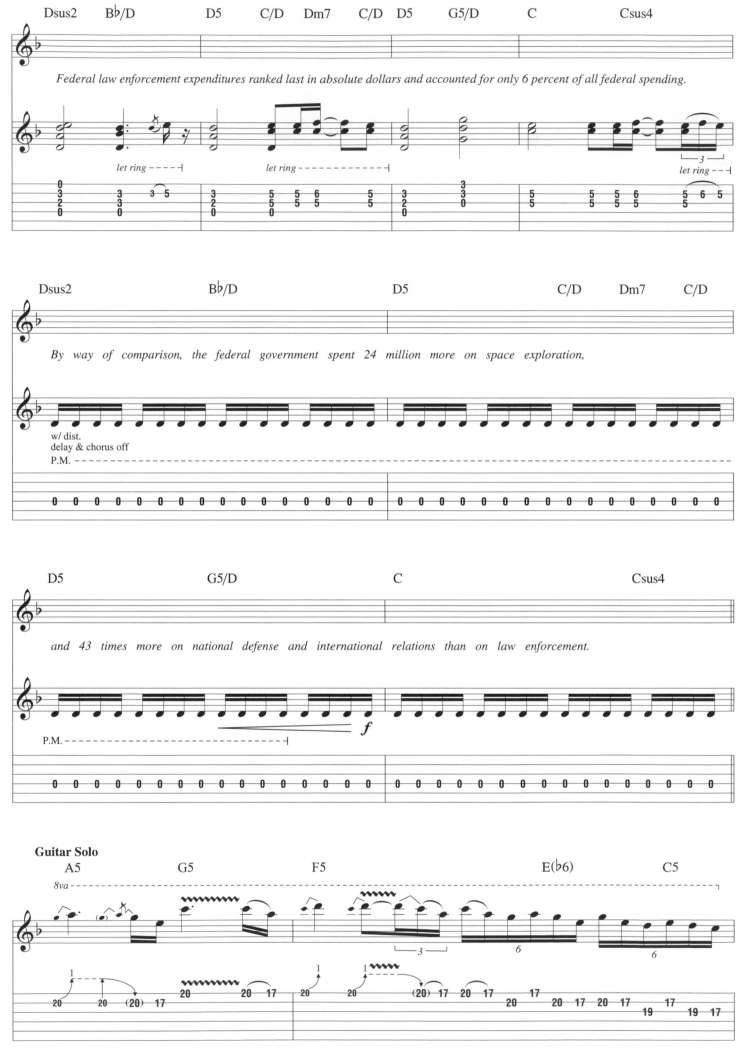

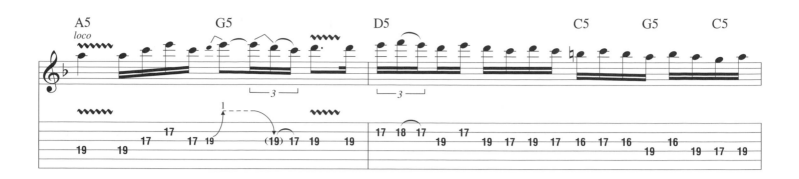

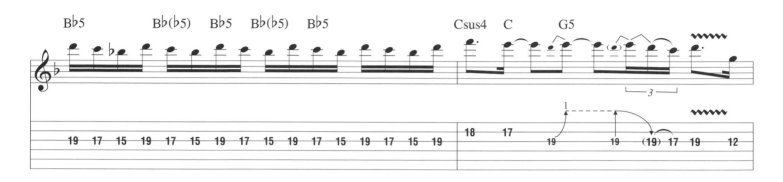

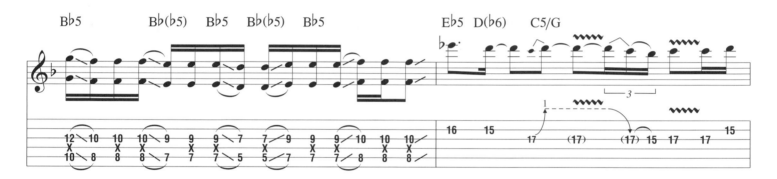

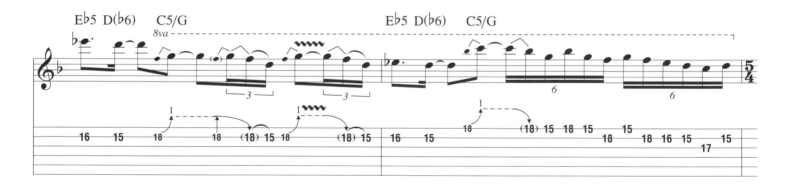

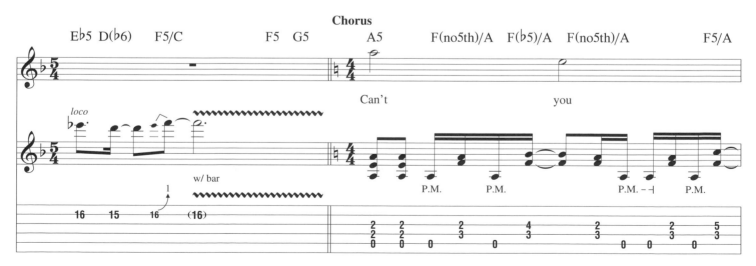

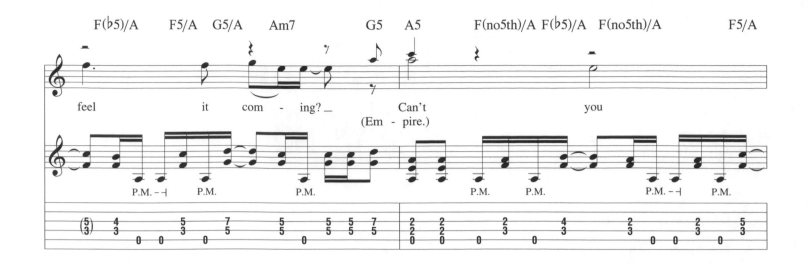

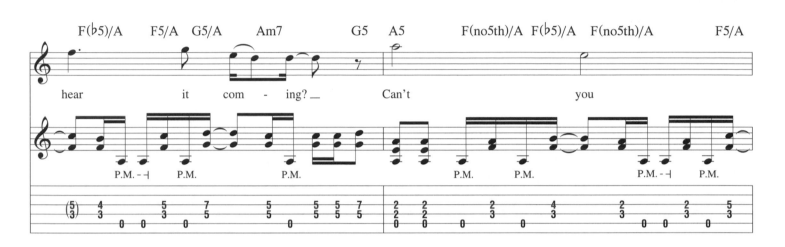

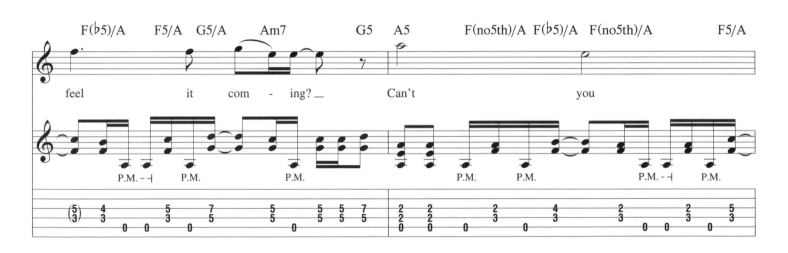

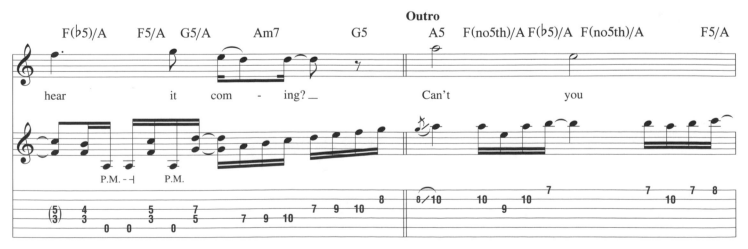

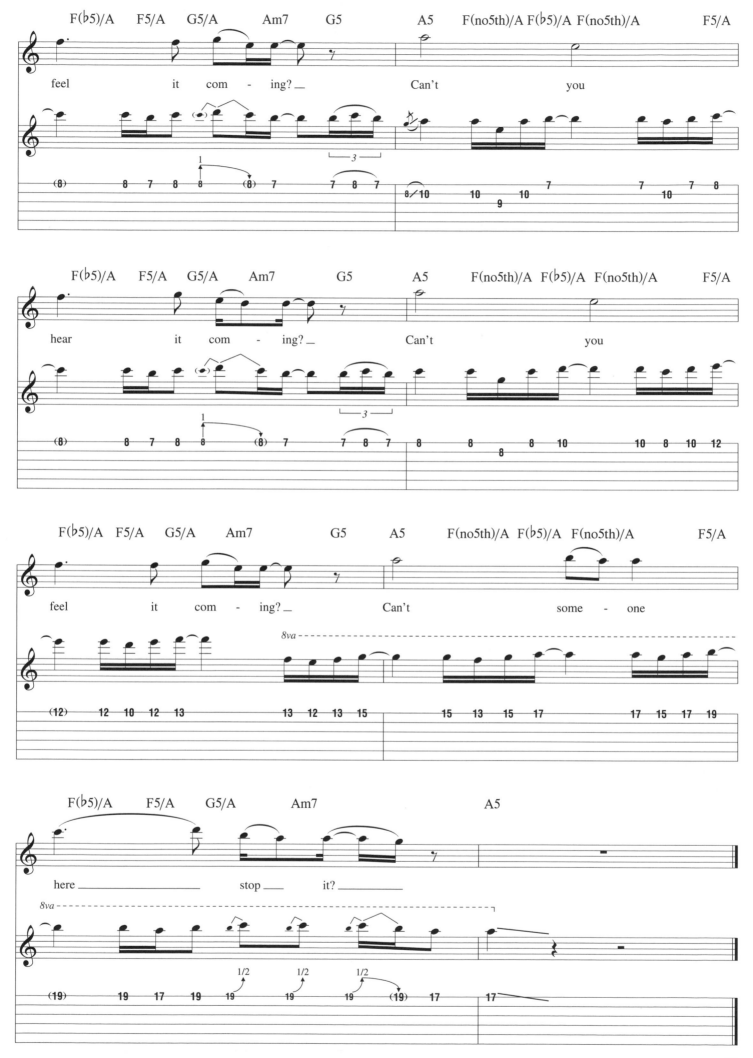

Push

Written by Rob Thomas and Matt Serletic

Tune down 1/2 step:
(low to high) Eb-Ab-Db-Gb-Bb-Eb

Intro
Moderately slow ♩ = 84

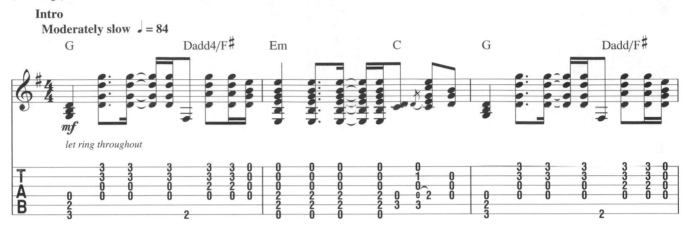

Verse

1. She said I don't know if I've ev-er been good e-nough.

I'm a lit-tle bit rust-y, and I think my head is cav - ing in. And

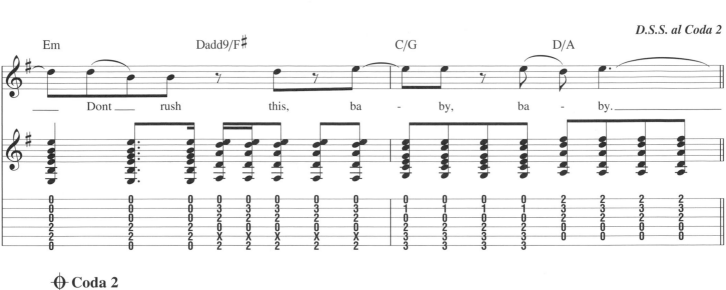

Coda 2

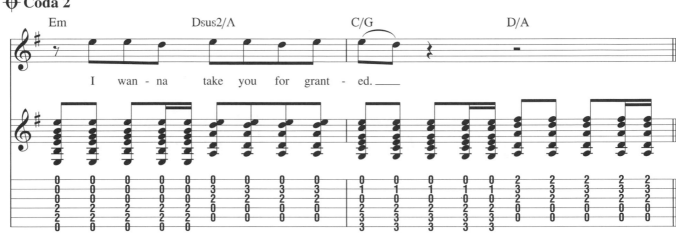

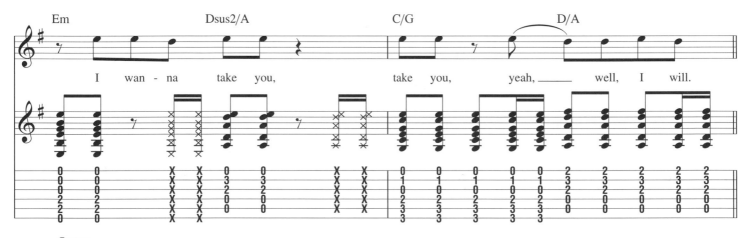

Outro

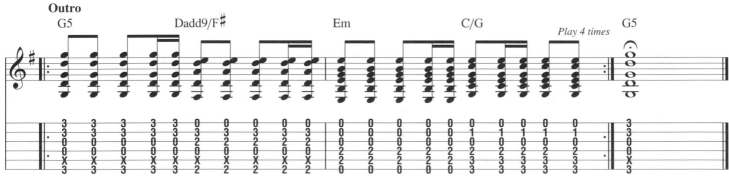

Additional Lyrics

Pre-Chorus Oh, well, don't just stand there,
Say nice things to me
'Cause I've been cheated, I've been wronged.
And you, you don't know me, yeah.
Well, I can't change.
Well, I won't do anything at all.

The Freshmen
Words and Music by Brian Vander Ark

Capo II

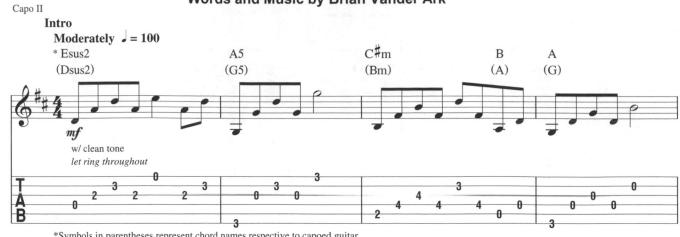

*Symbols in parentheses represent chord names respective to capoed guitar.
Symbols above reflect actual sounding chords. Capoed fret is "0" in tab.

1. When I was young, I knew ev-'ry-thing. She, a punk who rare-ly ev-er took ad-vice. Now I'm

guilt strick-en, sob-bing with my head on the floor. Stop a ba-by's breath, and a shoe-full of rice, __ now.

ev - er die for these sins. We were mere - ly fresh - men.

Interlude

2. My best

Verse

friend took a week's va - ca - tion to for - get her. His girl took a week's worth of

val - ium and slept. And now he's guilt strick - en, sob - bing with his head on the floor. Thinks _

*Notes to the right of slashes played by bass, next 5 meas.

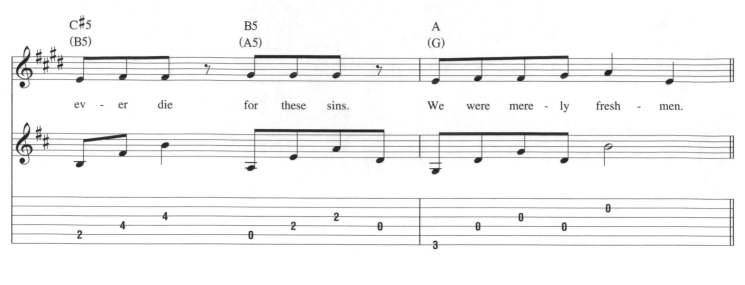

ev - er die for these sins. We were mere - ly fresh - men.

Outro

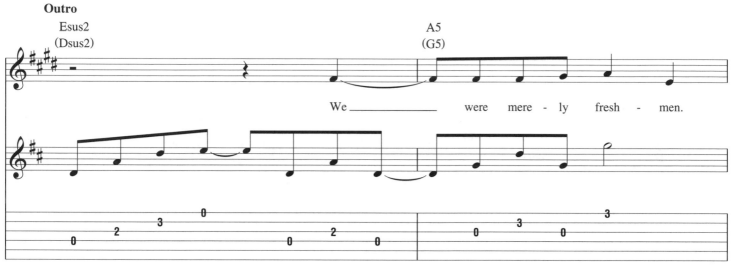

We _____ were mere - ly fresh - men.

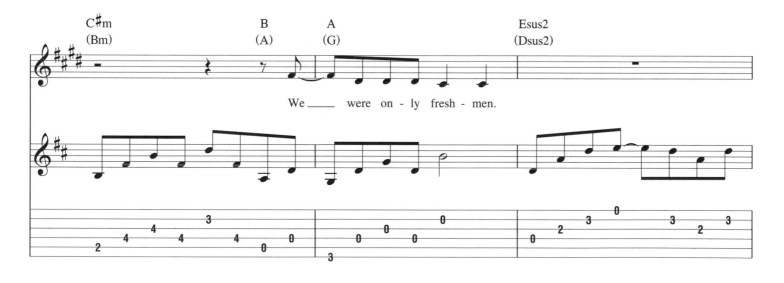

We ___ were on - ly fresh - men.

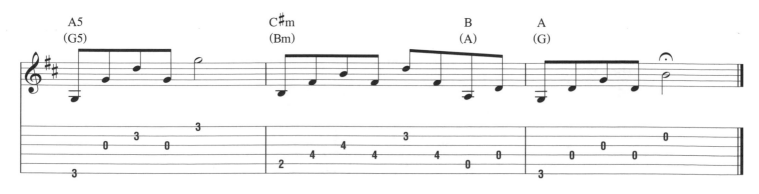

Interstate Love Song

Words and Music by Dean De Leo, Robert De Leo, Eric Kretz and Scott Weiland

Intro
Moderately slow ♩ = 84

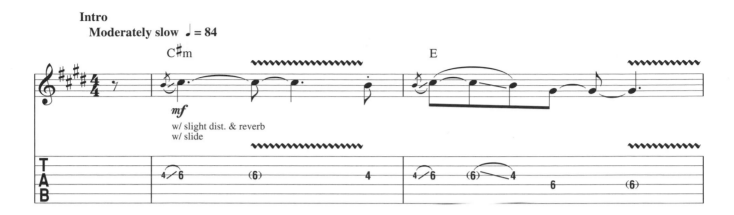

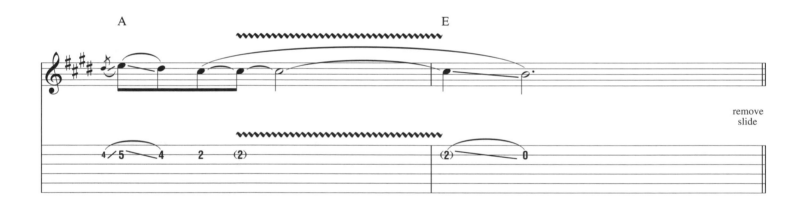

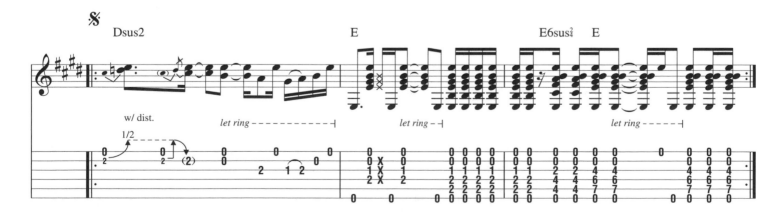

35

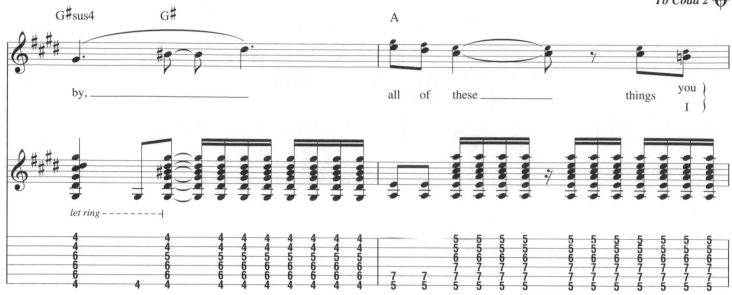

 Coda 1

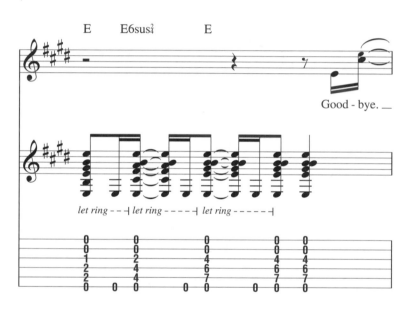

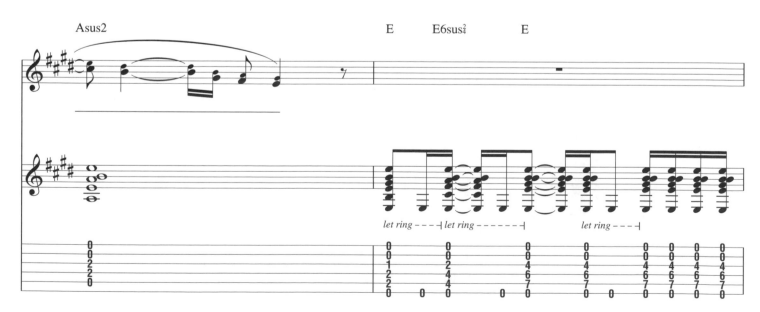

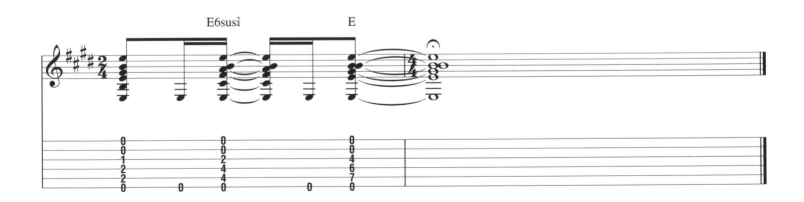

Additional Lyrics

2. Feelin', a, like a hand in rusted shame,
   So do you laugh or does it cry? Reply?

3. Breathin' is the hardest thing to do,
   With all I've said and all that's dead for you; you lied.

Mother

Words and Music by Glenn Danzig

Intro
Moderately ♩ = 128

Verse

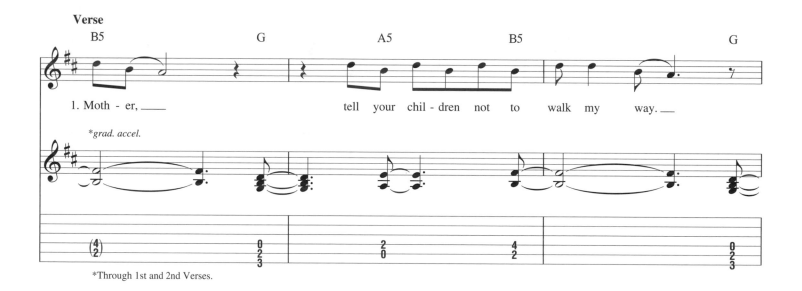

1. Moth - er, ____ tell your chil - dren not to walk my way. ____

*grad. accel.

*Through 1st and 2nd Verses.

Tell your chil - dren not to hear my ____ words, ____ what they mean, what they say.

⊕ Coda

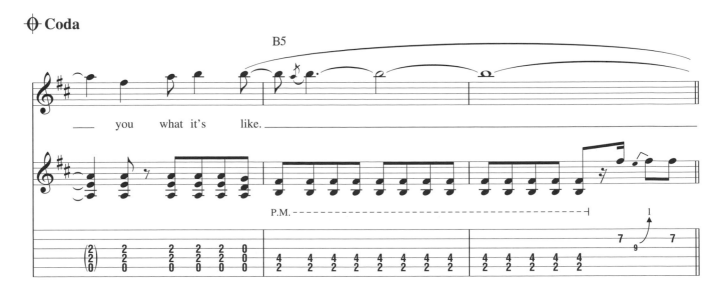

Outro-Guitar Solo

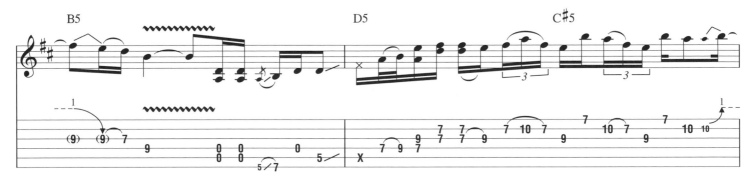

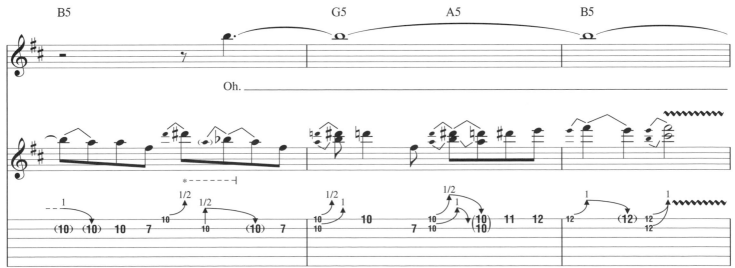

*Catch 2nd string under bending finger.

Additional Lyrics

3. Mother, tell your children not to hold my hand.
   Tell your children not to understand. Oh, mother.
   Father, do you wanna bang heads with me?
   Do you wanna feel ev'rything? Oh, father.

Mr. Jones

Words by Adam Duritz
Music by Adam Duritz and David Bryson

ing at you.___ Ah,___ no,___ no, she's look-ing at me."___ Smil - ing in the bright ___

___ lights   Com - ing through in ster - e - o   When

To Coda

ev - ery-bod - y loves _____ you,   you can nev - er be lone -

1.   2.   **Bridge**
                                            Half-time feel ♩ 70
                                            w/ Lead Voc. ad lib.

- ly ___   3. I ___   - ly _____

49

*T = thumb on 6th stg.

I want to be a li-on

Ev-ery-bod-y wants to pass __ as cats __

__ We all want to be big __ big stars, __ but we got dif-ferent rea-sons for that

Be-lieve __ in me __ Be-cause I don't be-lieve __ in an-y-thing and I __

We all want to be big stars, but we don't ___ know why and we don't ___

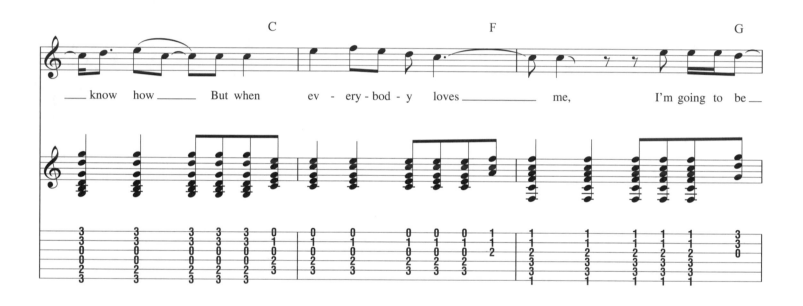

___ know how ___ But when ev - ery - bod - y loves ___ me, I'm going to be ___

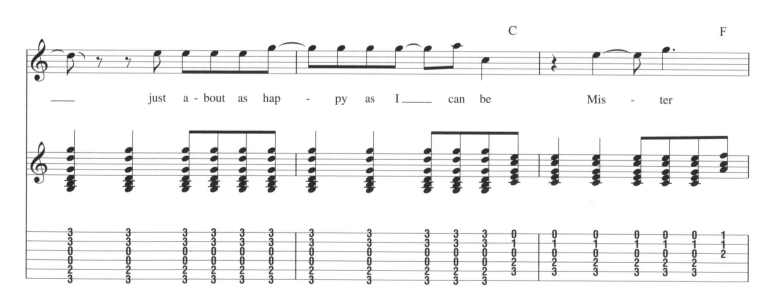

___ just a - bout as hap - py as I ___ can be Mis - ter

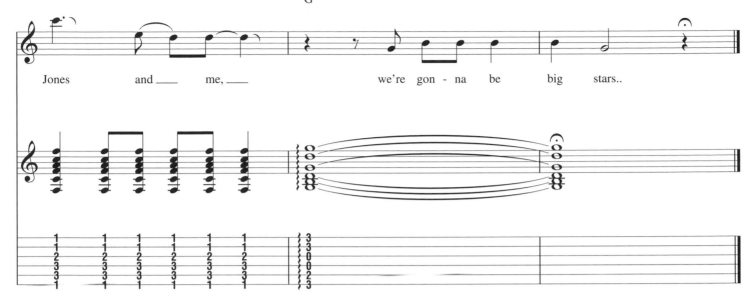

Jones   and ___ me, ___   we're gon - na   be   big   stars..

Additional Lyrics

3. I will paint my picture
    Paint myself in blue and red and black and gray
    All of the beautiful colors are very very meaningful
    Gray is my favorite color
    I felt so symbolic yesterday
    If I knew Picaso I would buy myself a gray guitar and play

Chorus 2. Mr. Jones and me look into the future
    Stare at the beautiful women
    "She's looking at you.
    Uh, I don't think so. She's looking at me."
    Standing in the spotlight
    I bought myself a gray guitar
    When everybody loves me, I will never be lonely

Chorus 3. Mr. Jones and me stumbling through the barrio
    Yeah we stare at the beautiful women
    "She's perfect for you, Man, there's got to be
    somebody for me."
    I wanna be Bob Dylan
    Mr. Jones wishes he was someone just a little more
    funky
    When everybody loves you, son, that's just about as
    funky as you can be

Yellow Ledbetter

Words and Music by Jeffrey Ament, Eddie Vedder and Mike McCready

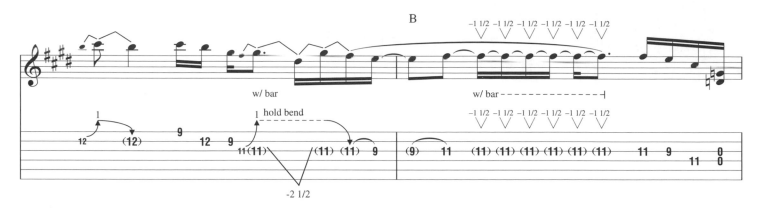

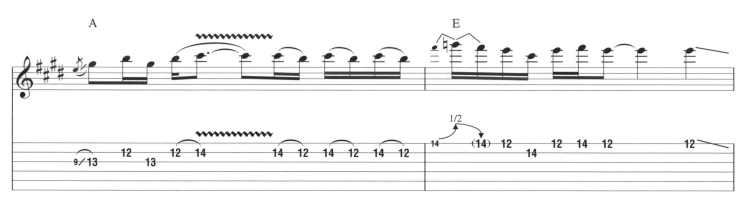

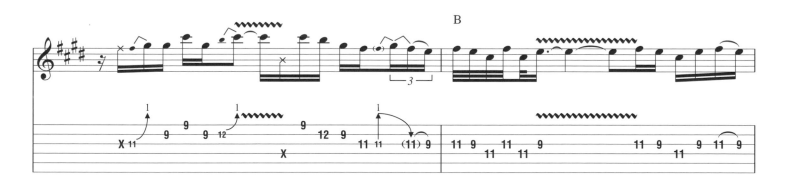

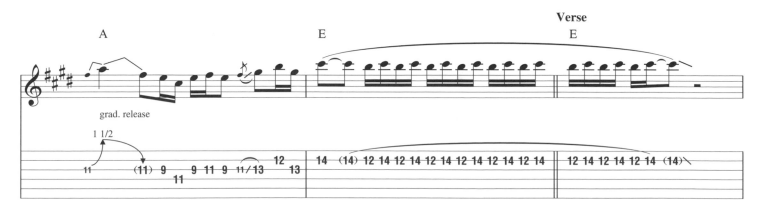

59

Outro

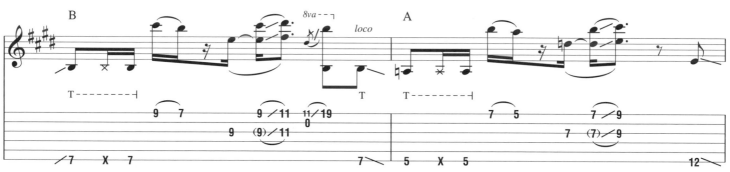

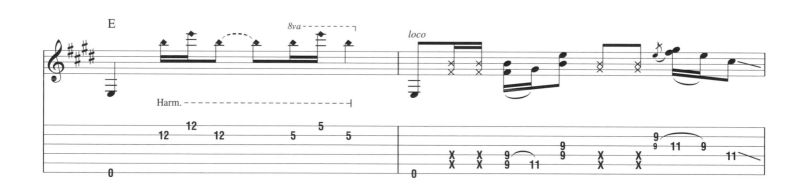

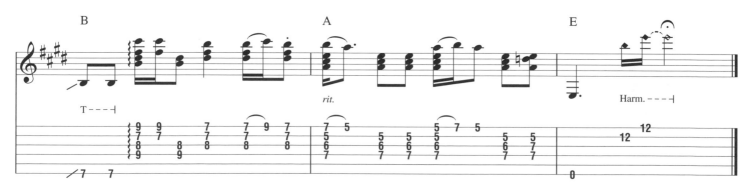

GUITAR NOTATION LEGEND

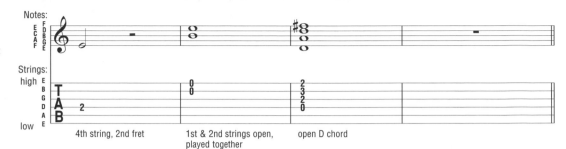

THE MUSICAL STAFF shows pitches and rhythms and is divided by bar lines into measures. Pitches are named after the first seven letters of the alphabet.

TABLATURE graphically represents the guitar fingerboard. Each horizontal line represents a string, and each number represents a fret.

4th string, 2nd fret

1st & 2nd strings open, played together

open D chord

HALF-STEP BEND: Strike the note and bend up 1/2 step.

WHOLE-STEP BEND: Strike the note and bend up one step.

GRACE NOTE BEND: Strike the note and immediately bend up as indicated.

SLIGHT (MICROTONE) BEND: Strike the note and bend up 1/4 step.

BEND AND RELEASE: Strike the note and bend up as indicated, then release back to the original note. Only the first note is struck.

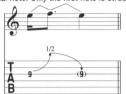

PRE-BEND: Bend the note as indicated, then strike it.

VIBRATO: The string is vibrated by rapidly bending and releasing the note with the fretting hand.

PALM MUTING: The note is partially muted by the pick hand lightly touching the string(s) just before the bridge.

HAMMER-ON: Strike the first (lower) note with one finger, then sound the higher note (on the same string) with another finger by fretting it without picking.

PULL-OFF: Place both fingers on the notes to be sounded. Strike the first note and without picking, pull the finger off to sound the second (lower) note.

LEGATO SLIDE: Strike the first note and then slide the same fret-hand finger up or down to the second note. The second note is not struck.

SHIFT SLIDE: Same as legato slide, except the second note is struck.

TRILL: Very rapidly alternate between the notes indicated by continuously hammering on and pulling off.

TAPPING: Hammer ("tap") the fret indicated with the pick-hand index or middle finger and pull off to the note fretted by the fret hand.

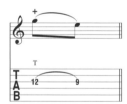

NATURAL HARMONIC: Strike the note while the fret-hand lightly touches the string directly over the fret indicated.

PINCH HARMONIC: The note is fretted normally and a harmonic is produced by adding the edge of the thumb or the tip of the index finger of the pick hand to the normal pick attack.

TREMOLO PICKING: The note is picked as rapidly and continuously as possible.

VIBRATO BAR DIVE AND RETURN: The pitch of the note or chord is dropped a specified number of steps (in rhythm), then returned to the original pitch.

VIBRATO BAR SCOOP: Depress the bar just before striking the note, then quickly release the bar.

VIBRATO BAR DIP: Strike the note and then immediately drop a specified number of steps, then release back to the original pitch.

Additional Musical Definitions

(accent) • Accentuate note (play it louder).

(staccato) • Play the note short.

D.S. al Coda • Go back to the sign (%), then play until the measure marked "***To Coda***," then skip to the section labelled "**Coda**."

D.C. al Fine • Go back to the beginning of the song and play until the measure marked "***Fine***" (end).

Fill • Label used to identify a brief melodic figure which is to be inserted into the arrangement.

N.C. • Harmony is implied.

• Repeat measures between signs.

• When a repeated section has different endings, play the first ending only the first time and the second ending only the second time.

HAL·LEONARD GUITAR PLAY·ALONG

This series will help you play your favorite songs quickly and easily. Just follow the tab and listen to the CD to hear how the guitar should sound, and then play along using the separate backing tracks. Mac or PC users can also slow down the tempo without changing pitch by using the CD in their computer. The melody and lyrics are included in the book so that you can sing or simply follow along.

INCLUDES TAB

VOL. 1 – ROCK	00699570 / $16.99	
VOL. 2 – ACOUSTIC	00699569 / $16.95	
VOL. 3 – HARD ROCK	00699573 / $16.95	
VOL. 4 – POP/ROCK	00699571 / $16.99	
VOL. 5 – MODERN ROCK	00699574 / $16.99	
VOL. 6 – '90s ROCK	00699572 / $16.99	
VOL. 7 – BLUES	00699575 / $16.95	
VOL. 8 – ROCK	00699585 / $12.95	
VOL. 9 – PUNK ROCK	00699576 / $14.95	
VOL. 10 – ACOUSTIC	00699586 / $16.95	
VOL. 11 – EARLY ROCK	00699579 / $14.95	
VOL. 12 – POP/ROCK	00699587 / $14.95	
VOL. 13 – FOLK ROCK	00699581 / $14.95	
VOL. 14 – BLUES ROCK	00699582 / $16.95	
VOL. 15 – R&B	00699583 / $14.95	
VOL. 16 – JAZZ	00699584 / $15.95	
VOL. 17 – COUNTRY	00699588 / $15.95	
VOL. 18 – ACOUSTIC ROCK	00699577 / $15.95	
VOL. 19 – SOUL	00699578 / $14.95	
VOL. 20 – ROCKABILLY	00699580 / $14.95	
VOL. 21 – YULETIDE	00699602 / $14.95	
VOL. 22 – CHRISTMAS	00699600 / $15.95	
VOL. 23 – SURF	00699635 / $14.95	
VOL. 24 – ERIC CLAPTON	00699649 / $16.95	
VOL. 25 – LENNON & McCARTNEY	00699642 / $14.95	
VOL. 26 – ELVIS PRESLEY	00699643 / $14.95	
VOL. 27 – DAVID LEE ROTH	00699645 / $16.95	
VOL. 28 – GREG KOCH	00699646 / $14.95	
VOL. 29 – BOB SEGER	00699647 / $14.95	
VOL. 30 – KISS	00699644 / $16.99	
VOL. 31 – CHRISTMAS HITS	00699652 / $14.95	
VOL. 32 – THE OFFSPRING	00699653 / $14.95	
VOL. 33 – ACOUSTIC CLASSICS	00699656 / $16.95	
VOL. 34 – CLASSIC ROCK	00699658 / $16.95	
VOL. 35 – HAIR METAL	00699660 / $16.95	
VOL. 36 – SOUTHERN ROCK	00699661 / $16.95	
VOL. 37 – ACOUSTIC METAL	00699662 / $16.95	
VOL. 38 – BLUES	00699663 / $16.95	
VOL. 39 – '80s METAL	00699664 / $16.99	
VOL. 40 – INCUBUS	00699668 / $17.95	
VOL. 41 – ERIC CLAPTON	00699669 / $16.95	
VOL. 42 – CHART HITS	00699670 / $16.95	
VOL. 43 – LYNYRD SKYNYRD	00699681 / $17.95	

VOL. 44 – JAZZ	00699689 / $14.95	
VOL. 45 – TV THEMES	00699718 / $14.95	
VOL. 46 – MAINSTREAM ROCK	00699722 / $16.95	
VOL. 47 – HENDRIX SMASH HITS	00699723 / $19.95	
VOL. 48 – AEROSMITH CLASSICS	00699724 / $16.99	
VOL. 49 – STEVIE RAY VAUGHAN	00699725 / $16.95	
VOL. 50 – NÜ METAL	00699726 / $14.95	
VOL. 51 – ALTERNATIVE '90s	00699727 / $12.95	
VOL. 52 – FUNK	00699728 / $14.95	
VOL. 53 – DISCO	00699729 / $14.99	
VOL. 54 – HEAVY METAL	00699730 / $14.95	
VOL. 55 – POP METAL	00699731 / $14.95	
VOL. 56 – FOO FIGHTERS	00699749 / $14.95	
VOL. 57 – SYSTEM OF A DOWN	00699751 / $14.95	
VOL. 58 – BLINK-182	00699772 / $14.95	
VOL. 59 – GODSMACK	00699773 / $14.95	
VOL. 60 – 3 DOORS DOWN	00699774 / $14.95	
VOL. 61 – SLIPKNOT	00699775 / $14.95	
VOL. 62 – CHRISTMAS CAROLS	00699798 / $12.95	
VOL. 63 – CREEDENCE CLEARWATER REVIVAL	00699802 / $16.99	
VOL. 64 – THE ULTIMATE OZZY OSBOURNE	00699803 / $16.99	
VOL. 65 – THE DOORS	00699806 / $16.99	
VOL. 66 – THE ROLLING STONES	00699807 / $16.95	
VOL. 67 – BLACK SABBATH	00699808 / $16.99	
VOL. 68 – PINK FLOYD – DARK SIDE OF THE MOON	00699809 / $16.99	
VOL. 69 – ACOUSTIC FAVORITES	00699810 / $14.95	
VOL. 70 – OZZY OSBOURNE	00699805 / $16.99	
VOL. 71 – CHRISTIAN ROCK	00699824 / $14.95	
VOL. 72 – ACOUSTIC '90S	00699827 / $14.95	
VOL. 73 – BLUESY ROCK	00699829 / $16.99	
VOL. 74 – PAUL BALOCHE	00699831 / $14.95	
VOL. 75 – TOM PETTY	00699882 / $16.99	
VOL. 76 – COUNTRY HITS	00699884 / $14.95	
VOL. 78 – NIRVANA	00700132 / $14.95	
VOL. 80 – ACOUSTIC ANTHOLOGY	00700175 / $19.95	
VOL. 81 – ROCK ANTHOLOGY	00700176 / $22.99	

VOL. 82 – EASY SONGS	00700177 / $12.99	
VOL. 83 – THREE CHORD SONGS	00700178 / $14.99	
VOL. 84 – STEELY DAN	00700200 / $16.99	
VOL. 85 – THE POLICE	00700269 /$16.99	
VOL. 86 – BOSTON	00700465 / $16.99	
VOL. 87 – ACOUSTIC WOMEN	00700763 / $14.99	
VOL. 88 – GRUNGE	00700467 / $16.99	
VOL. 91 – BLUES INSTRUMENTALS	00700505 / $14.99	
VOL. 92 – EARLY ROCK INSTRUMENTALS	00700506 / $12.99	
VOL. 93 – ROCK INSTRUMENTALS	00700507 / $14.99	
VOL. 96 – THIRD DAY	00700560 / $14.95	
VOL. 97 – ROCK BAND	00700703 / $14.99	
VOL. 98 – ROCK BAND	00700704 / $14.95	
VOL. 99 – ZZ TOP	00700762 / $14.99	
VOL. 100 – B.B. KING	00700466 / $14.99	
VOL. 102 – CLASSIC PUNK	00700769 / $14.99	
VOL. 103 – SWITCHFOOT	00700773 / $16.99	
VOL. 104 – DUANE ALLMAN	00700846 / $16.99	
VOL. 106 – WEEZER	00700958 / $14.99	
VOL. 108 – THE WHO	00701053 / $14.99	
VOL. 109 – STEVE MILLER	00701054 / $14.99	
VOL. 111 – JOHN MELLENCAMP	00701056 / $14.99	
VOL. 113 – JIM CROCE	00701058 / $14.99	
VOL. 114 – BON JOVI	00701060 / $14.99	
VOL. 115 – JOHNNY CASH	00701070 / $14.99	
VOL. 116 – THE VENTURES	00701124 / $14.99	
VOL. 119 – AC/DC CLASSICS	00701356 / $14.99	
VOL. 120 – PROGRESSIVE ROCK	00701457 / $14.99	
VOL. 123 – LENNON & MCCARTNEY ACOUSTIC	00701614 / $16.99	

Complete song lists available online.

Prices, contents, and availability subject to change without notice.

FOR MORE INFORMATION, SEE YOUR LOCAL MUSIC DEALER, OR WRITE TO:

HAL·LEONARD® CORPORATION
7777 W. BLUEMOUND RD. P.O. BOX 13819 Milwaukee, WI 53213

Visit Hal Leonard online at www.halleonard.com